Babylon
The Bitch

■ ■ ■

Enemy of Israel

By Prince Handley

University of Excellence Press

Copyright © 2014 by Prince Handley
All Rights Reserved.

UNIVERSITY OF EXCELLENCE PRESS
San Diego ▪ London ▪ Tel Aviv

ISBN-13: 978-0692319109
ISBN-10: 0692319107

Printed in the U.S.A.

Third Edition

The only *Babylon* book you need!

TABLE OF CONTENTS

FOREWORD

It has been estimated that the Nazi Holocaust killed one Jew in three. The worst is yet to come. **The next—and, soon coming—Holocaust will take two out of three Jews.**

"And it shall come to pass, that in all the land, says the LORD, two parts therein shall be cut off and die; but the third shall be left therein." Tanakh: Zechariah 13:8

This book discusses in detail how the enemy of Israel—Satan—will try to juxtaposition Babylon (a real city) in opposition to Jerusalem: both spiritually and physically.

Most people do NOT realize that the KEY enemy of Israel has clandestine architectural and strategic, as well as spiritual, plans against Israel. Plans that **include much more than Iran or ISIS or the UN.**

This is NOT just a juxtaposition of position, but of timing as well. Referencing the not-so-distant *End Time* prophetic events—*real time, real events*—with the present geopolitical landscape, you will learn:

 ■ The soon coming—*the worst*—Jewish Holocaust;

 ■ Babylon—*New World Order substitute*—for Jerusalem; and,

 ■ The only game plan—*that will work*—for Israel.

4

Babylon
The Bitch

Enemy of Israel

■ ■ ■

GEOPOLITICAL INTEL

It has been estimated that the Nazi Holocaust killed one Jew in three. The worst is yet to come. **The next—and, soon coming—Holocaust will take two out of three Jews.**

"And it shall come to pass, that in all the land, says the LORD, two parts therein shall be cut off and die; but the third shall be left therein." – Tanakh: Zechariah 13:8

This book discusses in detail how the enemy of Israel—Satan—will try to juxtaposition Babylon (a real city) in opposition to Jerusalem: both spiritually and physically.

If you understand this, you will be kilometers **ahead of the world think tanks**. Plus, you will have a perspective from which to **analyze** real-time prophetic issues. Then, **you can act accordingly**.

This is NOT just a juxtaposition of position, but of timing as well, referencing the not-so-distant *End Time* prophetic events—*real time, real events*—with the present geopolitical landscape. You will learn:

■ The soon coming—*the worst*—Jewish Holocaust;

■ Babylon—*New World Order substitute*—for Jerusalem; and,

■ The only game plan—*that will work*—for Israel.

In August, **2008** I warned Israel NOT to be deceived by (then) current peace talks by Olmert and Assad. At that time Obama and USA wanted to force Israel into negotiations with Damascus. I warned Israel—and Bibi Netanyahu specifically—NOT to do it. Listen to (or read show notes of) my podcast: "Israel, New Forces in Middle East Parlance."

After all my **suggestions and warnings to Israel for the last 10 years to strike Iran before it's too late**, I have been waiting in the wings watching. Like I said, Iran would play the "time" game. **Iran is in a BETTER position militarily now** as a result of Israel's non-action—and the USA's non-help diplomatically. Israel should have followed my several admonitions to take a preemptive strike against Iran.

What most people do NOT realize is that **the KEY enemy of Israel has clandestine architectural and strategic—physical AND spiritual—plans against Israel**. These plans **include much more than Iran**. They include much more than the Islamic–Iran–Turkey complex that will come against Israel (see Ezekiel Chapter 38 in Tanakh). These plans include much more than Hezbollah, ISIS, al-Qaeda, Hamas and other terrorist groups ... even more than the United Nations.

This book will show you WHO and WHAT will be in opposition to Israel—**even after Israel defeats the hordes form the North who come against her in Ezekiel 38**. Lots of people—even Bible prophecy teachers—confuse the battle described in Ezekiel 38 with the battle of Armageddon described in Revelation Chapter 19. **The groups (nations) fighting are**

7

different … and the instruments of war used to bring victory to Israel are different in each scenario.

This purpose of this book is to reveal the "subtle" plans being implemented and waiting for Israel in the End Times. **These are geopolitical schemes—traps in waiting—for Israel and the Jewish People.** For a specific blueprint of ALL the events leading up to the Time of the End, read and study, *Map of the End Times* and *Flow Chart of Revelation*, both by Prince Handley. (Both are available at Amazon and other book stores.)

With this introductory background information, we will now reference the not-so-distant **End Time** prophetic events—*real time, real events*—with the present geopolitical landscape, and expose the, up-to-now, **hidden Enemy of Israel in the End Times: Babylon, the Bitch**.

In my book, *Action Keys for Success*, I warn people: **"Your weakest moment will be after your success!"** And that—even after all the years Israel has suffered and endured victoriously, back in the land and with the **future** victory of Ezekiel 38 under her belt with God's help—will be her weakest moment … unless she listens to the warnings and suggestions in this book. Here we go … listen up!

THE NEXT JEWISH HOLOCAUST

There are several reasons WHY Satan is so focused on the destruction of Israel and the Jewish People.

א G-d loves the Jews and He loves Israel. In Torah, God says concerning Israel, *"For you are a holy people to the LORD your God: the LORD your God has chosen you to be a people for Himself, a special treasure above all the peoples on the face of the earth."* [Deuteronomy 7:6]

"The LORD did not set his love upon you, nor choose you, because you were more in number than any people; for you were the fewest of all people: But because the LORD loved you, and because he would keep the oath which he had sworn unto your fathers, (Abraham, Isaac and Jacob) has the LORD brought you out with a mighty hand, and redeemed you out of the house of bondmen, from the hand of Pharaoh king of Egypt." [Deuteronomy 7:7]

ב It was through the Jewish people that G-d inspired and gave the world the Holy Bible: the Tanakh (Jewish Old Covenant) and the Brit Chadashah.(Jewish New Covenant). [The *Book of Luke* in the New Covenant may have been written by a Gentile but we do not know for sure.]

ג It was through the seed line of the Jewish people from which Mashiach was born. Both Yosef and Miryam's family trees trace back to King David. Yosef (the husband of Miryam) has his family line going back to Solomon, son of King David. [See Brit Chadashah, the *Book of Mattiyahu (Matthew)* Chapter One, verses 1 – 17.] Miryam—*the virgin-maiden who conceived miraculously by the Ruach HaKodesh*—has her seed line on her father's side going back to Nathan, son of King David. [See the *Book of Luke*, Chapter Three, verses 23 -31.] Miryam's family tree was recorded—as was Jewish custom—on the men's side of the family, so it started with Yosef's father-in-law, Eli. [**Editor's Note**: Verse 23,*"Yeshua was about thirty years old when he began his public ministry. It was supposed that he was a son of Yosef who was of Eli."*]

At any time, anyone who opposed Yeshua—*concerning him being the Messiah*—could have gone to the Temple (similar to local courthouse records today) and proven Him false if He were. That was one thing of which the religious leaders NEVER accused Yeshua. His credentials were EXACT: Messiah, Son of David.

ד It was the Mashiach of Israel who HEALED the separation between God and man as a result of Adam's "fall" in the Garden of Eden. The eternal BLOOD of the Everlasting Covenant paid for the sins of a race fallen by the sin from Adam. The Lamb of

God—Mashiach—took our sins upon Him [*as Isaiah the Prophet foretold 700 years before*] and ... **"by His stripes we are healed."**

*"But he was wounded for **our** transgressions, he was bruised for **our** iniquities: the chastisement of **our** peace was upon him; and with his stripes we are healed."*

*"In fact, it was **our** diseases he bore, **our** pains from which he suffered; yet we regarded him as punished, stricken and afflicted by God. But he was wounded because of **our** crimes, crushed because of **our** sins; **the disciplining that makes us whole fell on him**, and **by his bruises [stripes] we are healed.**"* [Tanakh: Isaiah 53:4-5]

His blood was holy. He was perfect God and perfect man. Born of a virgin—**through a miracle of the Ruach HaKodesh**—His blood did not contain sin from an earthly father in Adam's seedline. Yeshua came from the Father God. To this Man **the ancient Rabbis testify**. This blood from the Lamb of God, **poured out for me and for you,** is sufficient atonement—payment and covering—for our souls. [Torah: Leviticus 17:11]

ה **Messiah will NOT come** [return again] **until Israel acknowledges Him and invites Him—*pleads with Him*—to come and bring deliverance. Then, the Deliverer will come to Zion. It is very plain ... If Satan**

can wipe out the Jews and Israel, the Mashiach can NOT return! <<< Think about it!

"I will go and return to my place, till they acknowledge their offence, and seek my face: in their affliction they will seek me earnestly." [Tanakh: Hosea 5:15]

The "affliction" spoken of will be the **Time of Jacob's Trouble.** *"Alas! for that day is great, so that none is like it: it is even the time of Ya'akov's [Jacob's] trouble; but he shall be saved out of it."* [Tanakh 30:7] **This will be last half (42 months) during the Seven Year Covenant that Israel will make with the Palestinians.** At the very end of the seven years Mashiach will return **when the Jewish people invite Him—*plead with Him* —to return.** Those last three and one-half years (42 months) of the Seven Year Peace Treaty **will be worse than the Nazi Holocaust ...** especially for those Jews living in *Ezor Yehuda VeShomron – Judea and Samaria area, or West Bank.*

Every Israeli—and every Jewish person—should read, ***Map of the End Times***, and study also the companion book, ***Flow Chart of Revelation***. Both of these books are available at Amazon and other book stores in both e-Book and Paperback. (See back page for info.)

I When Messiah comes—as King—He will destroy the enemies of Israel and set up His earthly

12

Kingdom, ruling from Jerusalem. He will deliver His people.

"In that day the LORD will defend the inhabitants of Jerusalem ... It shall be in that day that I will seek to destroy all the nations that come against Jerusalem." [Tanakh: Zechariah 12:8-9]

"I will destroy the strength of the goyim kingdoms." (Tanakh: Haggai 2:22]

*"And I will pour upon the house of David, and upon the inhabitants of Jerusalem, the spirit of grace and of supplications: and **they shall look upon me whom they have pierced**, and they shall mourn for him, as one mourns for his only son, and shall be in bitterness for him, as one that is in bitterness for his firstborn."* [Tanakh: Zechariah 12:10]

"And one will say to him, *'What are these wounds between your hands?'* Then he will answer. *'Those with which I was wounded in the house of my friends.'"* [Zechariah 14:4]

"In that day there shall be a fountain opened to the house of David and to the inhabitants of Jerusalem for sin and for uncleanness." [Zechariah 13:1]

So now you know **WHY** Satan hates the Jews and Israel:

א God loves the Jews and He loves Israel.

ב It was through the Jewish people that God inspired and gave the world the Holy Bible.

ג It was through the seed line of the Jewish people from which Mashiach was born.

ד It was the Mashiach of Israel who who HEALED the separation between God and man as a result of Adam's "fall" in the Garden of Eden.

ה Messiah will NOT come [return again] until Israel acknowledges Him and invites Him—**pleads with Him**—to come and bring deliverance. Then, the Deliverer will come to Zion. If Satan can wipe out the Jews and Israel, the Mashiach can NOT return!

ו When Messiah comes—as King—He will destroy the enemies of Israel and set up His earthly Kingdom, ruling from Jerusalem.

Now you know WHY the Jews—and Israel—have suffered and been opposed so much throughout history. And now you know WHY the Jews are back in Eretz Israel after nearly 2,000 years of dispersion. It is time **soon** for Mashiach to come to Israel and set up His

14

Messianic Kingdom. But—before He returns—the worst Holocaust the Jews have ever experienced will happen: the Prophet Jeremiah called it the **Time of Jacob's Trouble**.

What you are seeing and hearing in the news is the "sign" of the preparation of Israel for a great spiritual awakening in which multitudes of Jews turn to Mashiach Yeshua during the worst Holocaust the Jews have ever known.

BABYLON, CAPITAL OF THE NEW GLOBAL GOVERNMENT

Islam will likely be the catalyst which will bring about the one world government. Muslim terrorism is now global. You will begin to see the loss of your right to privacy. Israel and the USA will be the key targets of this attack. Islamic terrorism will be the active agent to frighten people into wanting New World Governance.

The Qur'an instructs Muslims to kill non-Muslims (Jews and Christians). In exchange for being allowed to build her Temple, Israel will sign a peace treaty with the coming world leader: the **false**-messiah. We will review the historic world powers and their treatment of Israel ... and **how New Babylon will arise** from a 10 region cooperative of leaders who give support to the coming world leader: the false Mashiach.

Babylon—the Bitch—is just that! I am going to show you certain details of the harlot Babylon that are NOT covered by usual theological exegesis. **Babylon, as in the past—so in the future—is the enemy of Israel AND is about to appear on the scene.**

HER ORIGIN

A summary of the the historic temporal or civil powers of the world is as follows:

א The first Babylonian Empire was founded by Nimrod. From the people of this empire, come ALL the empires of the world. God confounded the language of the people and scattered them abroad to his predetermined boundaries of ethnicity (the nations). (Torah - Genesis 11)

ב The people of Israel were set apart by God. Bible prophecy deals with the nations as they affect the Israelites (or the nation of Israel) in one way or another.

ג The first major empire to persecute Israel was of course Egypt. This empire was NOT included in Daniel's prophecy.

ד The second major empire to persecute Israel was Assyria. It was by Assyria that the Israelites of the northern Kingdom of Israel were taken into captivity. This empire was NOT included in Daniel's prophecy.

ה The third major empire which persecuted the

Israelites was the **second Babylonian Empire**. It was under this empire that the Israelites in the southern Kingdom of Judah were taken into captivity. **This empire was the FIRST in Daniel's series of four kingdoms**. You can read this in the Tanakh, in the *Book of Daniel*, the Prophet, Chapter Two. **It was represented by the head of gold**.

Note: The reason **Daniel started with the second Babylonian Empire** was that **this was during his lifetime** and **pertained to the interpretation of dreams and dream-visions that dealt with this empire and subsequent empires up to the end times**.

I The fourth major empire and the **SECOND** in Daniel's series of four kingdoms was **Medo-Persia**. **It was represented by the breast and arms of silver.**

T The fifth major empire and the **THIRD** in Daniel's series of four kingdoms was **Greece**. **It was represented by the belly and thighs of brass.**

N The sixth major empire and the **FOURTH** in Daniel's series of the four world kingdoms was the **Roman Empire. It was represented by the legs of iron … and NEXT …**

U. The feet part of iron and clay in Daniel's vision represent a revived Islamic Caliphate in the latter days ... (of which we have entered).

It's interesting to note that the etymological use of **"arab"** refers to the *"mixed people to the East of Israel."* Iron and clay do NOT mix.

REMEMBER THIS SUMMARY OF HISTORIC POWERS – YOU WILL NEED THEM LATER.

THEY ARE BABYLON'S "DBA'S"

IT IS A KEY TO THE SEVEN (7) HEADS OF THE SYSTEM UPON WHICH BABYLON OPERATES!

Most students of Bible prophecy agree now that in the last days there will be a **reconstituted, or revised, Islamic Caliphate**. This is mostly because of the dream-visions and interpretations in *Daniel* Chapters Two and Seven. Many liberal and neo-orthodox theologians attempt to discount the validity of Daniel as a prophet; however, **Yeshua (Jesus) gave validation to Daniel's prophetic office** when He, as Israel's Messiah, taught concerning the last days [Matthew 24:15 and Mark 13:14]. Mashiach Yeshua (Messiah Jesus also referred to the Prophet Daniel in His teaching, thereby giving validity to Daniel as a prophet.)

Many conservative or evangelical scholars surmised in the past that the geo-political area encompassed previously by the Roman Empire rule would be revived and be **the arena from which the anti-Christ, or false Messiah, would arise**. However, certain situations that are being played out today forge an entirely different set of circumstances while still emanating from the geographic confines of Eastern Europe (Turkey), the Middle East and North Africa.

May I suggest to you that the predominant force arising from the area of the Eastern extension of the old Roman Empire is none other than Islam, a religion spawned in Hell by Satan: a religion based upon the teachings of a deceived and false prophet, Muhammad, and the false god—*the ancient moon god*—allah.

NOTE: The majority of soldiers in the Roman Army who destroyed Jerusalem and the Temple in 70 AD / CE **were from Syria, Egypt and Arabia**. They were transcripts. **These were "the people of the prince who shall come" described in Daniel 9:26. Therefore, the "prince who shall come"**—*the anti-Christ*—**will be from the Middle East.**

The geographic confines described are composed of parts of **Eastern Europe, the Middle East and part of North Africa** (Libya and North Sudan) and **will be the sling from which the false-messiah—or, the anti-Christ—will be thrust**. He could likely be of Syrian Greek background.

20

The main point to realize, however, is that **Islam will likely be the catalyst which will bring about the New World Governance**. Let me explain:

א Muslim terrorism is now global.

ב Pertaining to people in the USA, they are already beginning to see the loss of their right to privacy. The Department of Homeland Security and The Patriot Act, even though established out of NEED and for the GOOD of the populace, are still instruments that can and may one day be used for invasion of privacy of Jews and Christians.

ג Islam is the #1 force in the drive to one world government. Islamic terrorism will be the active agent to frighten people into wanting a one world governing body.

People around the world will want peace and safety and will be willing to give up their governmental or constitutional rights for it. **This will be the caveat for the Jews and Israel when the coming world leader (chosen by the New World Governance) tricks Israel into signing a seven (7) year treaty with the conciliation that Israel can build the Temple**. However, it will be

21

with a great price. *"For when they shall say, 'Peace and safety,' then sudden destruction will come upon them, as travail upon a woman with child."* Daniel the Prophet and Jeremiah also spoke about this.

People will say, *"Give me peace—leave me and my money alone—and let me enjoy life."*

T Muslim terrorism is being used in the media to EQUATE to fundamentalism. Just the other day I heard a news commentator say that "there are fundamentalists in all religions" . . . and used the example of "Christian fundamentalists." Even fiction books now equate evangelical Christianity—and, also, Orthodox Judaism—with Islamic "fundamentalism."

The Koran (Qur'an) instructs Muslims to kill non-Muslims, and this especially promotes an anti-Jewish and anti-Christian concept! Christian fundamentalism AND Jewish fundamentalism, especially Hasidic and Orthodox Jews, will not only be the targets of Islam, but of an ever increasing cross section of global society. Born-again (real) Christians will not be persecuted because they are Christians, but because they are considered **fundamentalists ... terrorists** by society at large; likewise Hasidic and Orthodox Jews.

Question: Why is ISIS allowed to do their terrible acts of torture and murder without a great international outcry from the UN, but Israel is reprimanded for defending herself against rockets from Hamas in Gaza!

Yeshivas, seminaries, Jewish and Christian publishers, church movements are **selling out** and have embraced themselves in the tentacles of the **one world religion**. One major evangelical seminary recently accepted government money but had to sign an agreement that they would no longer teach students to convert Muslims. Churches are conducting surveys asking people what they should throw out or add in to get people in the community to come to church. Be careful when the world loves the church!

Over thirty years ago Francis Schaeffer said, *"Americans, just like Germans in the days before the Nazis, will be influenced to give up their constitutional privileges in exchange for (personal) peace (or, affluence)."* What he was saying is that Americans will give up their freedom that was bought with the blood of their relatives and forefathers because they don't want their life styles to be disturbed. They want to be at peace!

Dr. Robert Morey believes that **this may be the LAST generation of Americans that knows freedom and the first that knows tyranny (via the courts, legislation, and martial forces)**. He states, *"We are* *living in a watershed moment of history like an ostrich!"* And may I say here that **Israel needs to wake up and stop giving in to the demands of the Palestinians, the Arabs, the UN, the EU, NATO, The Hague and the USA.**

Next, I want to talk to you about the **identity** of Babylon, the Bitch. Also, I will describe to you her **support system**. And then, I will share with you **how she will be destroyed**.

HER IDENTITY

"And there came one of the seven angels which had the seven vials, and talked with me, saying unto me, Come here; I will show unto you the judgment of the great whore that sits upon many waters:

With whom the kings of the earth have committed fornication, and the inhabitants of the earth have been made drunk with the wine of her fornication.

So he carried me away in the spirit into the wilderness: and I saw a woman sit upon a scarlet colored beast, full of names of blasphemy, having seven heads and ten horns.

And the woman was arrayed in purple and scarlet color, and decked with gold and precious stones and pearls, having a golden cup in her hand full of abominations and filthiness of her fornication:

*And upon her forehead was a name written, **MYSTERY, BABYLON THE GREAT, THE MOTHER OF HARLOTS AND ABOMINATIONS OF THE EARTH.***

And I saw the woman drunk with the blood of the holy people of God, and with the blood of the martyrs of Yeshua (Jesus): and when I saw her, I wondered with great admiration."

— Brit Chadashah: Revelation 14, verses 1-6

There are seven keys to identifying Babylon, the Bitch. That is, there are KEY scriptural descriptions which inform us as to her geopolitical operations and location.

The Ruach Ha Kodesh—the Holy Spirit—revealed these to me years ago. I had never heard anyone teach about them and I had never read anything written by scholars about these keys. Almost every religious book, article, or commentary only described her as a religious system with origin and practices evolving from the ancient Babylon. However, **notice the following in Revelation Chapters 17 and 18** of the Brit Chadashah (the New Covenant, or New Testament):

א **Babylon is a literal city.** (Revelation 17:18 & 18:19)

ב **Babylon influences the leaders of the nations**. (Revelation 17:2, 18)

ג **Babylon involves the nations and their inhabitants with fornication**. (Rev. 17:2) Note: the word "fornication" is the Greek "porneuo" which can mean sexual trade (also human trafficking) or "illicit sexual intercourse or prostitution," and **is used both literally** (Mark 10:19, 1 Corinthians 6:18 & 10:8, Revelation 2:14 & 20) **and metaphorically** to describe spiritual

26

fornication, or idolatry; i.e. **false—anti God—religion, such as Islam**.

ד **Babylon is a seaport city.** (Revelation 18:17-19)

ה **Babylon is responsible for the murder of God's prophets and all who are slain upon earth.** (Revelation 17:6 & 18:24)

ו **Babylon is a key distributor of sorcery.** Sorcery can mean narcotics, witchcraft (magic arts) ... or idolatry, including spiritual delusion. (Revelation 18:23)

ז **Babylon is THE KEY CENTER of world trade**. (Revelation 18:9-1)

HER SUPPORT SYSTEM

We read that Babylon, the Bitch, rides upon—or is supported by—a system which has an historical and sequential background. That system is described as a "scarlet beast which was full of names of blasphemy, having seven heads and ten horns." (Rev. 17:1-3)

In Revelation 17:10 we read of seven (7) heads or kings, **five (5) of which are already fallen in Yochanan's (John's) day when he wrote the Book of Revelation**, one which John said "IS" (in his day, the #6), and the other **(the seventh) would rule AFTER** John lived. And, the seventh world power will last for a short while.

NOTE: The 7th kingdom will rule **in the future from the geographical confines of the old Eastern Roman Empire (Turkey), the Middle East and North Africa ... for a little while.**

Remember our summary above of the historic temporal or civil powers of the world?

KEY TO UNDERSTANDING THE SEVEN (7) HEADS OF THE SYSTEM UPON WHICH BABYLON—*THE BITCH*—OPERATES! HER CLANDESTINE "DBA'S"

The seven (7) heads are:

א Egypt

ב Assyria

ג Babylon (the second Babylonian Empire)

ד Medo-Persia

ה Greece

ו Rome (in Yochanan's day while writing the Book of Revelation)

ז A revived Islamic Caliphate in the latter days ... (of which we have entered).

The sixth major empire and the FOURTH in Daniel's series of four kingdoms was Rome. This was the head, or king, that Yochanan said "IS" (in his day, the #6) ... which was Rome (the Roman Empire). **The term "kings" is used in scripture different times to mean a dynasty or series of kings in a dynasty**, such as Jeremiah 25:11-12 ... and can also represent the **kingdoms** over which kings rule.

The beast (the anti-Messiah or false messiah) that **was** and **is not**, is himself also an **eighth** king, and is **of the seven**; and he goes into perdition. [Revelation 17:10-11] This is a perfect description of the anti-Messiah who will come to rule (7th), and then die with a deadly wound to the head, and then seemingly be raised to life again (8th). [Revelation Chapter 13]

The anti—*false*—messiah, will come from the geopolitical **"10 Region Islamic Confederacy"** confines of any of the following: Turkey, the Mediterranean countries ... including North Africa ... and the Middle East.

Remember, there was an Eastern extension of the Old Roman Empire (with its capitol in the area today known as Turkey) which outlasted the Western Roman Empire by 1,000 years (from the 4th Century to 1453 C.E.). Therefore, the **false** Messiah **can** emerge from either the Eastern EU, Mediterranean countries or Islamic countries in the Middle East.

The false Messiah (leader of the New World Governance) **will then select the religious leader of the world—the false prophet**—who may be **a Muslim Imam and a member of the Islamic Caliphate.**

As I mentioned, **Babylon, the Bitch, rides upon—or is supported by—a system which has a historical and sequential background.** That system is described as a

30

"scarlet beast which was full of names of blasphemy, **having seven heads and ten horns**."

The ten (10) horns of the beast upon which Babylon, the Bitch, rides **are ten regional leaders which will rule concurrently (at the same time) the False Messiah rules**. NOTE: **These ten kings are DIFFERENT from the seven dynasty kingdoms** (or, HEADS) on the beast. The ten horns are NOT sequential dynasties but rule at the same time in the ONE WORLD GOVERNMENT ... and at the same time as the anti-Messiah. (Revelation 17:12-13)

Ten regional leaders—heads of governments—will arise during the same time period. These ten world **regional** leaders will receive power during the same time period as the coming World Leader ("The Beast"). The ten leaders will have "one mind" and will give their power and strength unto the False Messiah: the anti-Christ ("The Beast").

These ten world leaders will have power on earth, but they are NOT from the earth. They are extra-terrestrial creatures. How do we know? Revelation 17:14 says, *"These shall—at the very end of the last three and one-half years—make war with The Lamb."* The Lamb is Yeshua HaMashiach (Jesus, the Messiah) who will come to deliver Israel at the Battle of Armageddon. No earthly king or leader could oppose the Messiah when he returns. **Only stupid demonic beings of the**

"spirit" world who follow Satan would attempt such an act.

Also, consider this about the ten "regional" leaders who will arise during the Time of the End. **The development of a hybrid species in the end times**—through which the anti-Christ MAY derive his submissive leadership core—**could well be the result of fallen spirit forces (demons) facilitating the same**, rather than aliens from another planet.

These fallen spirit forces (demons) may be from extra-dimensional time-space: not from other planets, but from a megaverse (outside our traditional concept of space-time continuum).

Some feel these will be willing subjects of alien abduction who receive genome altering implants. <u>I do NOT believe so</u> (however, it is a possibility). **There are other more scripturally based options as to HOW people may receive the genome altering implants or hybridization**.

Much research is being carried out today in areas of development of a "hybrid" species: i.e., harvesting of human fetuses and, also, **genetic modification**. Remember, there was gene pool corruption in Noah's day which resulted in God destroying the whole earth by the Great Flood; only 8 righteous souls were left: Noah, his wife, his three sons and their wives.

The "sons of God" took wives of those whom they chose. (Notice: the "sons of God" never refers to "believers" in the Tanakh, the Old Testament.)

1 Peter 3:19-20, 2 Peter 2:4-5 and Jude 6 refer to the fallen angels who procreated with the daughters of man in the Days of Noah (before the Flood). This resulted in the **Nephilim**: "the fallen ones"—or—"ones who cause others to fall." We know from scripture that the "fallen angels" who took to themselves the "daughters of men" (associated time wise with the Days of Noah and the Great Flood) have been bound in everlasting chains for their just judgment of everlasting fire.

NOTICE: **the offspring of the fallen angels**—the Nephilim—**were drowned in the Great Flood**. That is, their **bodies drowned;** however, **their spirits could be demons** we read about in the New Testament). **Demons never die!**

REPEAT: The development of a hybrid species in the end times—through which the anti-Christ MAY derive his submissive leadership core—could well be the result of fallen spirit forces (demons) facilitating the same, rather than aliens from another planet. **These fallen spirit forces (demons) may be from extra-dimensional time-space: not from other planets**, but from a megaverse (outside our traditional concept of space-time continuum).

33

HER DESTRUCTION

Remember ... the ten (10) horns of the beast upon which Babylon, the Bitch, rides are ten (10) kings which will **rule concurrently (at the same time) the anti-Messiah rules**. Let me repeat: **These ten kings are DIFFERENT from the seven dynasty kingdoms (or, HEADS) on the beast**. The ten horns are NOT sequential dynasties but rule at the same time in the one world New Global Governance—AND at the same time—as the **False** Messiah. (Revelation 17:12-13)

In other words, **the SUPPORT SYSTEM for Babylon will be the coming ONE WORLD SYSTEM ruled by the FALSE Messiah—or, pseudo-Christ—**[the 8th head from the previous 7th head] who arises from the confines of the old Roman Empire. The ten regional leaders will receive their authority for a while with the beast (the anti-Messiah).

These ten regional leaders **are of one mind** and will give their power and authority to the Beast: the FALSE Messiah. In other words, they will yield to him and acknowledge him as world leader through a legal pact. (Revelation 17:13)

➡➡➡ The **Ten Nation Islamic Confederacy**, its association with Babylon in Mecca, and **the influence of Turkey today will evolve into these ten regional Islamic regions.**

These ten regional leaders will later turn and hate Babylon, the Bitch, and destroy her, burning her with fire (probably as a result of nuclear attack). This is another way we know that Babylon is a LITERAL CITY. (Revelation 17:16-17 & 18:8-10)

These ten kings will also make war with Mashiach (that's a laugh). And, of course, they will be destroyed. Realize that God has put it in the hearts of the ten regional leaders to fulfill his purpose: to be of one mind, to give their kingdom to the beast, and to destroy Babylon, the Bitch! (Revelation 17:12-18)

Be at peace! The false trinity—**1. Satan; 2. the False Messiah; and, 3. the False Prophet**—will all be tormented forever: and all who follow them and **take the mark of the Beast.**

The Beast—*the anti-Christ governmental head of the New World Governance*—**his False Prophet**—*the religious head of the New World Governance*—**and** later **Satan,** himself—*the deceiver*—**will be cast into the lake that burns with fire**: forever and ever, time without end!

SUMMARY

If you have studied physics, you know that in our lifetime, earthly gold **has a half life** that will not wear out. However, on the time scale of God, earthly gold has a half life that wears out.

Messiah taught *us: "I counsel you to buy of me gold tried in the fire, that you may be rich; and white raiment that you may be clothed, and that the shame of your nakedness does not appear, and anoint your eyes with eye salve, that you may see."*

THE HARVEST RAIN HAS NEVER BEEN SEEN IN THE EARTH . . . ONLY THE FORMER RAIN! (See the Tanakh, Joel 2:23) Again, the Father's time scale is different than ours. **It is time to use your faith! The feast of the final harvest is soon!**

Hard times are coming for the Zion; however, those who know their God, and serve Mashiach, will experience supernatural MIRACLES.

It is time to reach Muslims, Buddhists, Hindus and the New Age world. People must see MIRACLES!

You, who are reading this book and who know HOW to operate in the Gifts of the Spirit should start praying for God ordained opportunities to pray for people. **Pray for**

their healing . . . lay hands upon them and loose the healing power of Messiah!

Also, you who are reading this book and who know HOW to intercede should start praying for **divine visitations** to people from the Lord. I know of MANY cases where Muslims have been saved because Messiah Yeshua appeared to **them in a dream, or a vision or in person**, and they were miraculously born again. (Several came to one of my seminars and have written me.)

Use your FAITH to loose the ministry of the holy angels. There is only ONE TRUE Messiah. And He is NOT a form of a devil named "Maitreya" or any other.

The Tanakh does not say that the earth will be filled with the knowledge of Islam, or Buddhism, or Hinduism, or New Age religion, but *"the earth shall be filled with the knowledge of the glory of the LORD, as the waters cover the* sea." (Habakkuk 2:*14)*

"Greater is He (God) that is in you than he (the devil) that is in the world."

● WHAT'S A JEW TO DO "GAME PLAN"

Let's examine where we are at. Then, we can plan and prepare for where we are going! We are in the "forefront" of the End Times: the entrance to the Last Days.

Babylon—the Bitch—has been a Satanic spiritual opposition to Israel through the centuries, manifesting herself through governmental and religious entities. However, in the End Times, she will be manifest **also** as a literal geographic commercial entity—**a city and government**—in juxtaposition to Jerusalem: physically and spiritually.

It's interesting to note that **Saudi Arabia could be the future home of New Babylon**. Bab-Illah, literally means the Gate To Allah. Also **Bab-Illah literally means Babel**. This Bab-Illah is also a literal golden gate made of the purist of gold in the Kaaba at **Mecca**.

The Kaaba ("The Cube") also referred as Al Kaaba Al Musharrafah (The Holy Kaaba), is a building at the center of Islam's most sacred mosque, Al-Masjid al-Haram, **in Mecca**, al-Hejaz, Saudi Arabia. It is the most sacred Muslim site in the world.

The black silk covering over the Kaaba is embroidered with verses of the Qur'an, made of the purest silver and gold, and decorate the dress with names of **blasphemy against the Son of God and the Trinity**.

Israel needs to use discernment and stand in opposition to any nation, government or entity that would try to take away her land ... which is rightfully hers by: **1.** Victory in war; and, **2.** By promise of God.

Israel will WIN a decisive "hands down" victory over the armies from the North and their allies who attack her. According to the Tanakh in Ezekiel Chapters 38-39, Turkey, Iran (possibly Russia and some previous USSR block countries and maybe Germany)—Central Asia Minor, and probably Iraq and Syria—plus two North East African regions **will attack Israel to take "spoil" and "plunder" her**.

➡ ➡ ➡ **At the time of attack Israel will be wealthy** and God uses her wealth as a "hook in the jaw" of the above mentioned attackers to "draw them" to attack her. WHY is this? It is because the LORD is going to magnify Himself and be sanctified—set apart—among the goyim (the nations) with such a MIRACLE victory. It will be as when God brought His People out of Egypt. **There will be NO doubt that the LORD God of Abraham, Isaac and Jacob is the God of Israel: the ONLY true God**.

Notice, the weapons God will use in this battle are: flooding rain, great hailstones, fire and brimstone (possibly a reference to nuclear munitions in the hand of Israel, also). **These weapons of warfare are different than those used in the End Time FINAL battle (the "so called" Battle of Armageddon) where Mashiach returns and defeats the enemies of Israel whom Satan will enlist to fight against the LORD.** (See Revelation Chapter 19 in the Brit Chadashah.)

Notice this also: **the people fighting against Israel are different in the Ezekiel 38 conflict than those fighting in Armageddon.** Many people—even Bible prophecy teachers—fail to see this. BOTH **the nations** AND **the weapons used are different**. In Armageddon, Mashiach returns with His saints and destroys the leaders of the nations who have joined themselves against national Israel, which undoubtedly will include **the combined military forces of the New Global Governance—successor to the New World Order and United Nations**.

The reason I have gone into a short replay of the Ezekiel 38 conflict is to allow you to realize that **AFTER this great victory for Israel**—over Turkey, Iran and their allies—**Israel still has her BIG "age old" enemy to watch out for: Babylon, the Bitch.**

I prophesy to Israel, to her people and her leaders: be aware of the whole End Time scene. You can NOT rest until Mashiach returns ... and He will return!

We know the following:

▪ There will be a seven year peace treaty between Israel and Palestinians.

▪ Israel will be allowed to rebuild her Temple on or near the Temple Mount.

▪ Animal sacrifices will be resumed at the Temple.

▪ The 144,000 Jewish evangelists will be protected by God as they prophesy (sometime after the Seven Year Peace Treaty is signed).

▪ There will be TWO witnesses who prophesy from Jerusalem for three and one-half years (sometime after the Seven Year Peace Treaty is signed).

▪ There were be a legal underpinning of the New World Governance (NWG).

▪ There will emerge the leader of the **NWG**, who will be the False Messiah.

▪ The **False** Messiah (the Anti-Christ) will select the False Prophet (world religious leader).

■ In the middle of the seven years, the False-messiah will order the animal sacrifices to stop.

■ The **False** Messiah will go into the Temple and declare he is God. (Daniel 9:27 and Matthew 24:15]

■ The **False** Messiah is called that "abomination of desolation" that Daniel and Yeshua prophesied concerning.

■ After this, there will be 42 months of the worst Holocaust the Jews—and God's people—have ever known.

■ One-third of the world's remaining population will die (one-fourth already died).

■ This leaves only one-half of the world's population left.

■ During this time, Babylon will become the world center of commerce.

■ Babylon may evolve into a great seaport metroplex area. Mecca is 79 kilometers (49 miles) from the Red Sea now, and the Jeddah seaport on the Red Sea could be dredged in the future to accommodate increased international trade.

■ Babylon will be supported initially by a **10 region Islamic federation** similar to the *Organization of*

Islamic Cooperation [OIC].

▪ The final Organization of Islamic States [OIS} will eventually meld Sunnis, Shias and ISIS into one group - *but still separated internally.*

▪ Babylon will influence world leaders with: 1. Trade; 2. Immorality; and, 3. Bloodshed.

▪ Babylon will be burned and destroyed by nuclear attack from the same 10 regional leaders who initially supported her.

▪ Mashiach will return and destroy the enemies of Israel and set up His earthly Kingdom.

Here's what works. **Here's what a Jew** (or anyone) **should do to prepare**.

Make sure you know Mashiach personally. **Do NOT wait because there will be a strong delusion sent upon the earth and it will be too late then**. Pray this prayer:

"Father in Heaven, if Yeshua (Jesus) is really my Messiah, then reveal Him to me. I ask Jesus to come into my life right now and to help me live for Him. Please forgive my sins and take me to Heaven when I die. Amen!"

As we enter more into the End Times, there will be persecution and hard times for God's People. I have included some suggestions for you in the following paragraphs. I am assuming that you will be around for a while and that you—by the time you finish this book—will have made up your mind that **Israel WINS!**

Start home Bible studies. Ask the Ruach HaKodesh (Holy Spirit) to show you what to study from Torah, Tanakh, and Brit Chadashah. He will guide you into all truth.

You will want to develop and implement a network of home Bible study and prayer groups—people (haverim) you know—as there will be lots of spies and false believers—*government informers*—in the future. Also, you will NOT be able to meet openly in the coming days, especially if you know Yeshua (Jesus).

These study groups, or "cell" groups, will actually be home or clandestine synagogues or churches. **They will need to be mobile and flexible in meeting times, locations and activities**.

NOTE: I have helped people (new believers) take part in mikvah (water baptism) in oceans, rivers, streams, bathtubs—in the mountains, the desert, in snow and in rain—in daylight, at nighttime and in different countries. One time the ocean became like an underwater lighted swimming pool at Midnight—and it was NOT plankton—because the waters were dangerous and I asked God for help to see. I could see clearly the bottom of the ocean floor. I have never known anyone to catch a cold even when I baptized them in snow and ice in the winter. God blesses obedience!

You will probably, as the LORD leads you, want to have some sort of "independent" trade or profession. This way, you can be flexible in schedule while doing the will and work of the LORD. (Study the life of Rabbi Shaul—the Apostle Paul—in the Brit Chadashah.)

Also, by having your own source of income you will NOT be under the scrutiny of the "world system" as you would be as a full time employee of an organization. For years I have encouraged believers to **establish "secret societies" of tradesmen and professionals** to help underwrite and support the ministry of God's Prophets.

Remember that there are TWO elect groups in the end times, as we have shown above:

- The 144,000 Jewish evangelists; and,
- The two street preachers in Jerusalem.

You can help support the 144,000 Jewish evangelists—and others—in this special group that God has called. You may NOT know who the 144,000 are, but it is highly probable that God will reveal them to His People.

You will need to be aware of "normal" Messianic **organic**—Spirit directed—growth. When a NEW group of believers is established, the LORD raises up

Prophets and Teachers. Then the Ruach Elohim (the Spirit of God) **calls** Apostles: these are "sent ones" from the midst of the cell group. The believers "lay hands" on the Apostles ratifying the call of the Holy Spirit, and **gifts of the Spirit are imparted to the Apostles**. Then, the Apostles are sent out to establish NEW works, or cell groups.

NOTICE: It is the Holy Spirit who *calls* and the Holy Spirit who *sends* out the Apostles. In between the calling and sending is "**fasting**" and the "**laying on of hands**" by the leaders and members of the cell synagogue, where certain gifts of the Holy Spirit are imparted by either prophecy or laying on of hands or both. (Read in Brit Chadashah an account of this in the Book of Acts, Chapter 13: 1-4.)

Have a wonderful life serving God ... and show other people the Way. Here's a promise for YOU. I have seen many MIRACLES claiming this promise from GOD:

"Call to me and I will answer you, and show you great and mighty things which you do not know."
– Tanakh: Jeremiah 33:3

LIVE A LIFE OF EXCELLENCE!

ADDENDUM

Throughout this book we have followed normal hermeneutical procedures of Biblical interpretation:

Literal (unless obviously intended to be symbolic).

Historical (background, time and relationships).

Cultural (tribal, ethnic and societal norms).

Grammatical (original language as well as context).

Genre of the text (narrative, prophecy, history, poetry).

Intended meaning or purpose of the author (reason for writing).

Interpreting Scripture with Scripture (comparing other proof texts).

Each verse in the Bible has one unique interpretation only; however, that verse may have many applications. The one correct interpretation is that which reflects the intent of the writer.

In *Babylon the Bitch: Enemy of Israel* we have adhered to the Middle Eastern background, culture, historical setting and **purpose** of the consensus of authors within their day.

In the last 100 years, many—if not most—evangelical and conservative scholars have interpreted the following as representing Rome (the Roman Empire):

> Daniel Chapter 2 – the legs of iron (the 4th kingdom).
>
> Daniel Chapter 7 – a beast, dreadful and terrible (the 4th kingdom).
>
> Revelation Chapter 17 – the 6th king, the one who is in John's day.

Also, they have interpreted the following as representing an "extension" of the Roman Empire:

> Daniel Chapter 2 – **the feet and toes** (on the legs of iron) being **part of iron and part of clay.**
>
> Daniel Chapter 7 – **the ten horns** (of the fourth beast, dreadful and terrible).
>
> Revelation 17 – **the other** [7th] **king / kingdom that is not yet.**

Many—if not most—of these scholars assigned the "extension" of the Roman Empire described above as pertaining to a revived Roman Empire, specifically a 10 regional amalgamation of leaders from countries or areas that were included in the earlier (ancient) Roman Empire. Also, **in more recent years many have ascribed this revision or extension to the European Union (EU) ...** and out of which will arise the New World

Governance with the New World Leader: The Beast—*the false Messiah*—the anti-Christ.

Remember, as I have referenced earlier in this book, there was the **Eastern extension of the Roman Empire** that outlasted the previous, or Western Division, for another 1,000 years and included areas of **Turkey, the Middle East and North Africa**.

The problem with ascribing Rome to the placement of the fourth (**4th**) kingdom in Daniel Chapters Two and Four is that Rome never "crushed" the previous kingdoms of Babylon (**#1**), Medo-Persia (**#2**) and Greece (**#3**). Actually, Rome was—of sorts—beneficial in some respects as it implemented infrastructure and allowed various religions to practice their beliefs (as long as they were subservient to Rome).

Remember, Greek was the universal language of the day under Rome. Greek being the universal language of the day, along with the network of Roman roads—*All roads lead to Rome*—helped the Gospel to spread from Jerusalem outward.

The only empire of force that identifies with "crushing" the previous kingdoms was—and is—Islam. The Islamic Caliphate overtook and encompassed the land mass of Babylon, Medo-Persia and Greece combined. NOTE: Most of the Roman Empire's borders faded about 500 miles west of Babylon.

It is important to recognize that all of the prophets who wrote concerning the "evil personage" in the Last Days—referring to the false Messiah, or anti-Christ—were prophesying **in relation to Israel.** These authors, writing under the inspiration of the Ruach Elohim (Spirit of God), were **writing in the context of the Middle East.**

In this book we have also discussed how we believe the False Prophet will probably be an Imam from the Islamic Caliphate ... and probably be selected by the coming world leader, the Beast (the anti-Christ, or false messiah).

We have also directed the reader's attention to the prominence of Turkey NOW—and in the days ahead—and leading into the Great Tribulation, the Time of Jacob's Trouble (Jeremiah Chapter 30, Matthew 24:15-21, Daniel 9:27).

We have outlined that Babylon is likely to be the home of the New World Governance and **may be** in Mecca, Saudi Arabia. Bab-Illah, literally means the Gate To Allah.

Also **Bab-Illah literally means Babel.** This Bab-Illah is also a literal golden gate made of the purist of gold in the Kaaba at **Mecca**.

However, having studied the Scriptures daily for over 50 years, I must concede that there **may be** other options for the location of New Babylon. Let us review the following scriptures again **to help us identify Babylon**:

> 1. Babylon is a literal city. (Revelation 17:18 & 18:19)
>
> 2. Babylon influences the leaders of the nations. (Revelation 17:2, 18)
>
> 3. Babylon, the Bitch, influences national leaders and people worldwide with fornication—**possibly literal** (*including human trafficking*), **probably spiritual**—causing them to forsake God. (Rev. 17:2)
>
> 4. Babylon is a seaport city. (Revelation 18:17-19)
>
> 5. Babylon is responsible for the murder of God's prophets and people who are slain upon earth. (Revelation 17:6 & 18:24)
>
> 6. Babylon is a key distributor of **sorcery** which **can mean** narcotics, witchcraft (magic arts) … or idolatry, including **spiritual deception and delusion**. (Revelation 18:23)
>
> 7. Babylon is THE KEY CENTER of world trade. (Revelation 18:9-1)

There seems to be at first glance some **possible inconsistencies with the Babylon–Islamic interpretation**. For example:

1. Islam (even though a Satanic religion) is "religiously" against literal sorcery "narcotics and witchcraft."

2. Islam (even though a Satanic religion) is "religiously" against illicit sexual fornication plus pornography, sexual trade and idolatry.

3. Babylon is a seaport city.

As for the first seeming inconsistency (**#1**), Babylon could develop—as we discussed—into a very large megaplex, especially with dredging of the Jeddah–Red Sea port. And, with such a huge population—if the literal meaning of the word "sorcery" is intended—could be the home of cartels, covens and crooks.

The second inconsistency (**#2**) may easily be dismissed by the following: The word "fornication" is the Greek "porneuo" which can mean "illicit sexual intercourse or prostitution," and is used literally (Mark 10:19, 1 Corinthians 6:18 & 10:8, Revelation 2:14 & 20) **but can also be used metaphorically to describe spiritual fornication, or idolatry; for example a false—anti God—religion, such as Islam.**

As for inconsistency **#3**, we have already discussed the possibility of dredging of Jeddah at the Red Sea to facilitate increased international trade. Jeddah is only 66 km (41 miles) from Mecca.

One important thing to consider—as we discussed earlier—**Turkey is ONE KEY to End Time prophecy ...** and Turkey—*at this time*—is a close ally of Saudi Arabia.

However, to think creatively—*to defy dogmatism*—I **would like to propose other possible scenarios for the location of New Babylon**. Since we know from Revelation Chapters 17 and 18 in the Brit Chadashah that **Babylon is definitely a seaport city dealing in international trade**, it **could be** located geographically in such places as:

Istanbul, Turkey

Dubai, United Arab Emirates

New York, USA

Rotterdam, Netherlands

London, UK

Jeddah, Saudi Arabia

Possibly, Istanbul, Dubai, New York (home of UN), Rotterdam (near The Hague), London—*or other places*—could be contenders

Rotterdam, Netherlands. The Port of Rotterdam is **only 13 miles (20 kilometers) from The Hague**: The United Nations Court of Justice. This is also the home of the UN War Crimes Tribunal: [ICC] International Criminal Court.

However, keep I mind that one way to identify Babylon will be that it is a key distributor of **fornication and sorcery, either of which can have literal or spiritual meanings: or both!** Therefore, sexual trade along with narcotics and witchcraft **could be** included. However, **we can be assured**—due to Babylon's murder of God's prophets and people worldwide—that **the spiritual meaning is included**.

Which brings us, also, to the realization that Islam has been responsible—in the past and now in our day—for the beheading and murder of God's people worldwide.

IMPORTANT

Attempts to place New Babylon at locations other than a seaport city are NOT accurate Biblical interpretation.

SOMETHING ELSE TO THINK ABOUT

Prophecy is message concerning the future, and is sometimes fulfilled in multiple events and over a period of many years. For example, in Isaiah 7:14 and in Daniel Chapters 8 and 11.

Remember this always: The Holy Bible is Middle Eastern centric: **from Creation to the Second Appearing of Messiah Jesus.**

Our job is to search the scriptures diligently. Much has been revealed to us in recent years, especially since the start of the regathering of Israel in 1948, and much more will be revealed as we continue on.

We do know for sure that Satan will try to juxtaposition Babylon (a real city) in opposition to Jerusalem: both spiritually and physically.

Most people do NOT realize that **the KEY enemy of Israel has specific clandestine architectural and strategic**—*as well as spiritual*—**plans against Israel**. Plans that **include much more than Iran or ISIS or the UN.**

> *"Pray for shalom in Jerusalem;*
> *may those who love you prosper."*

Your friend,
Prince Handley

BONUS

To help you, and to help you teach others, we have prepared Rabbinical Studies at this site:

www.uofe.org/biblical-studies.html
(scroll down)

These are commentaries from **ancient** Jewish Rabbis that identify the Mashiach of Israel.

To help you, and to help you teach others, we have also prepared Bible Studies in **English**, **Spanish** and **French** on the same site as the Rabbinical Studies.

- English FREE Bible Studies

  www.uofe.org/biblical-studies.html

- Spanish FREE Bible Studies

  www.uofe.org/biblical-studies.html

- French FREE Bible Studies

  www.uofe.org/biblical-studies.html

ANNOUNCEMENT

We recommend you obtain the companion books to this book, *Map of the End Times* which discusses in detail **the End Time events** that will take place on Planet Earth. Also, *Flow Chart of Revelation*, which focuses on the "judgments" that will be unleashed on Planet Earth during the end times. It is an easy to follow **chronological flow** of the events described in *The Book of Revelation*.

You will need this information in the future! Also, you will want to obtain, *Prophetic Calendar for Israel and the Nations.* This book is **a prophetic outlook through 2023**.

And, for sure you will want to have *Enhanced Humans: Mystery Matrix* in your library. There is *at this time* a geopolitical "behind–the-scenes" collusion, both human and other-worldly, that is being orchestrated to facilitate **control** … of YOU and your family … and of Israel.

+

All these books are available at Amazon and other book stores. (See the last page for Order information.)

UNIVERSITY OF EXCELLENCE PRESS
Los Angeles ■ London ■ Tel Aviv

NOTE

For seminars with Prince Handley, contact:

mentorhelp@gmail.com

OTHER BOOKS BY PRINCE HANDLEY

- Map of the End Times
- How to Do Great Works
- Flow Chart of Revelation
- Action Keys for Success
- Health and Healing Complete Guide to Wholeness
- Prophetic Calendar for Israel & the Nations: Thru 2023
- Healing Deliverance
- How to Receive God's Power with Gifts of the Spirit
- Healing for Mental and Physical Abuse
- Victory Over Opposition and Resistance
- Healing of Emotional Wounds
- How to Be Healed and Live in Divine Health
- Healing from Fear, Shame and Anger
- How to Receive Healing and Bring Healing to Others
- New Global Strategy: Enabling Missions
- The Art of Christian Warfare
- Success Cycles and Secrets
- New Testament Bible Studies (A Study Manual)
- Babylon the Bitch – Enemy of Israel
- Resurrection Multiplication – Miracle Production
- Faith and Quantum Physics – Your Future
- Conflict Healing – Relational Health
- Decision Making 101 – Know for Sure
- Total Person Toolbox
- Prophecy, Transition & Miracles
- Enhanced Humans – Mystery Matrix
- Israel and Middle East – Past Present Future
- Anarchy and Revolution: A Prophecy
- Real Miracles for Normal People
- Sexual Immorality: Addiction of Loss
- Healing Toolbox Plus: A to Z Workshop

AVAILABLE AT AMAZON AND OTHER BOOK STORES

UNIVERSITY OF EXCELLENCE PRESS
San Diego ■ London ■ Tel Aviv

www.ingramcontent.com/pod-product-compliance
Lightning Source LLC
Chambersburg PA
CBHW060611030426

42337CB00018B/3038